www.finishinglinepress.com

Downtown

ACKNOWLEDGMENTS

For Eva, for Ella, for Cody

Publisher: Leah Maines

Editor: Christen Kincaid

Cover Art: Nicole Callihan

Author Photo: Amanda Field

Cover Design: Elizabeth Maines McCleavy

Printed in the USA on acid-free paper.
Order online: www.finishinglinepress.com
                also available on amazon.com

Author inquiries and mail orders:
Finishing Line Press
P. O. Box 1626
Georgetown, Kentucky 40324
U. S. A.

"Poor thing. To die and never see Brooklyn."
—Anne Sexton

After the fog rolls out, the clouds roll in. I pin a bird to my shirt and take the elevator down to the earth.

I cannot see my hand in front of my face.

There is a loveliness in, finally, encountering so many disgraceful appetites.

In the sky, I had imagined a man would knock on my door and offer me coffee. When there was nothing, I went to forage.

Where I'm from, God is the one we think will come for us. He is the kindliest with his sad blue eyes and his soft gray hair.

By the time I reach the avenue, it's raining. I'm soaked. I cup my hands and drink the water. I pretend that this gesture might save me.

As the shopkeepers unlatch their metal gates, I say mean things to my reflection.

Bitch, fat ass.

I am hungry, too.

The bird will not stay fixed. I walk back and forth along the avenue where teeth are being sold, and when the gentlemen say dirty things to me, I blush.

Hey baby. Mama, honey, lick.

I am my only danger.

In the park, the children climb on me and call me base. Mama is base, they yell.

I should be grading, be in Paris, be at Trader Joe's.

Milk, wine, flowers.

I can't let you leave me not knowing what a fragment is, I tell Yi Jing. He is so human. In office hours, I like to reach my hand for him and watch him flinch.

From the clouds dangles the long rope of a crane.

One Christmas I was back in Oklahoma, and in front of the pink hospital where my mother worked, there was a crane with lights in the shape of a heart. I sat in the parking lot and wept for all the poets who had ever died. This was before robots.

The sheer number of bad ideas I have is striking.

On the avenue, a teenage boy wears a giant clock around his neck.

Heart. Crane.

Woman's talking, she says: I can't teach you to be a man. I'm a total bitch. Then she looks at me. What you looking at, bitch?

The sky, usually the sky. Or some disembodied digitalized version of my little tiny world.

There is a photograph of a man standing in front of a blue wall in Marrakech. I like to imagine I know him.

The women online say that what I am feeling is normal.

In Norman, there were shooting stars and rainbows and Derek Joe who played his guitar and drew me pictures of bugs crawling out of people's eyeballs. I think this was before he gave me scabies but maybe it was after.

My husband says, my grandmother is here, can't you do your poetry thing another day?

No. No, no, no, no. But the grandmother is dying (even more so than I am) so maybe I will.

On the avenue, the gentlemen hum hallelujah and offer me fliers for gospel music concerts.

In the sky, I need things. I never needed flowers when I lived close to the ground, but now I'm always standing in line at Trader Joe's with a fistful of calla lilies.

My favorite way to live as a child was in secret. I was so good at it no one ever even knew.

Tick tock. Tick tock.

Last night I went to a gala. My twin sister was being honored. She wore leopard. I wore black. I had forgotten I have a twin because she lives in another part of town. I groaned about midlife while she smoked a cigarette and checked her lipstick.

On the avenue, the language is much more colorful than it had been on the block. I look at my six year-old to see if she hears. She seems not to.

When I got my period, I was ten and didn't know what it was. I steeled myself for death.

Thank you for your support, both moral and financial.

At the gala, my twin sister receives a pink Statue of Liberty trophy. Pink. There are rich people, and there are artists. The artists do strange dances on stage; the rich people try not to look at their phones. Someone calls the "work" "daring".

That I drink too much is not my worst vice.

Thank you for your support, both financial and moral.

In her first grade class, my daughter is developing a character called "Me." Me's likes include doggies; her dislikes, homework and butts.

What are you doing here?

Deleted things still live on. I miss the days when words just disappeared.

The Bachelorette is sitting prettily in my DVR. All day, my thoughts wander back to her. Will she find love?

I had snuck out of the house wearing a dirty shirt. Seventh grade. All I wanted was to dance with Chad Harrington. He said, you stink. I stunk. I was wearing a dirty shirt. Maybe it was just the shirt that stunk but it was rubbing off on me.

At the gala is a man who sells terry cloth blazers for ONE THOUSAND DOLLARS. I tell him I will help with marketing. So: would you like to buy a blazer? Can people who read poetry afford ONE THOUSAND DOLLAR blazers? I hope so! They are perfect for St. Barthes. You can BASK in them.

In St. Martin, we saw rainbows every day, and our host smelled like the very best weed. We said, "I moustache you a question" with increasing regularity.

Are you twins?

Can you be trusted?

I moustache you: how much are the teeth?

My teeth came out very late. I was ten with huge boobs and a couple of missing teeth and a big OLE Southern accent. MORNING Y'ALL!!!

On the school bus to the farm, I hold a bag of little girl vomit.

In the sky, I can't sleep. Walruses only sleep for ninety seconds at a time. This is me. I keep waking up to press my face to the glass.

I feel so terrible and so lucky all the time.

The three year-old is starting to draw circles. I fear for her fine motor skills. For a little while, I let this be my greatest fear.

Knock. Knock.

My therapist asks me to consider what the horses do.

In order to better understand the man who stands in front of the blue wall, I ask my twin sister to call him. He is the only person in the free world who still answers his phone.

I make Yi Jing diagram sentences with me. The light at this time of day is just right for this sort of thing.

Hey, he says.

This is what we see at the farm: one rooster among twenty hens, a pink pig named Kevin who does not come when called, a horse all by her lonesome.

I like to drink Big Gulps. Multiple Big Gulps in a single day. Mostly, I blame the crazy thirst. I keep hoping I'll run into the old mayor, and he'll physically restrain me.

When Jesus made wine from water, the apostles said, Hallelujah.

Words that start with a include apple, angst, angle, angry, ankle.

K asks if I'm feeling sad, but I'm not. Just anxious. Especially when I dream I can't move my legs. Just thinking about those dreams makes me not able to move my legs.

Still, I walk the avenue. I walk the avenue in cowboy boots and a rain slicker, even though the day is hot and sunny. People on the avenue don't care. They are yelling at each other, not at me.

The artists at the gala wear whiteface. They dance. I try to dance too but my legs won't work. Instead, I talk to my twin who is carrying around her pink trophy. People keep interrupting us to congratulate her. Towards the end of the night, we dial numbers.

Is your refrigerator running?

I am so embarrassed I want to throw up. This is what I am thinking as I hold the bag of little girl vomit.

Where I'm from, God sees everything.

I hadn't wanted to worry my mother. I hadn't wanted to say: I am bleeding and will be dead by year's end.

The six year-old is all questions. What if day was night and night was day?

What if our house is really ice and just melts away?

What if all the glass breaks?

My husband's face is in a rectangle. He says he misses us but then we get cut off.

Oh my little buttercup, what will become of us?

I cannot tell where the bird has flown.

I cannot tell whether O has won the lottery or lost everything, but probably it is both. Probably it is always both.

And what is it my therapist wants me to say when she asks what the horses would do? Eat grass? Wander forever in circles?

This is where the subject goes, and this is where you put the verb.

Back on the block, I order Rosé with S.

Things are not what they seem!

We opt for martinis instead. I lie to her about lots of things. The babysitter needs to leave, I say, but really I want to watch the Bachelorette. I am doing okay, I say, but really I keep sticking screws into my skin and twisting them in.

But things are REALLY not what they seem!!!

We order another martini. I let her yell into the well that is me. I post a picture of her where she looks wildly, brilliantly, beautifully happy, and then we cry into our vodka-filled french champagne glasses which she tells me were first modeled after Marie Antoinette's small, perfect breasts.

Clink clink!!!

On the avenue, walking home, the gentlemen say nothing to me. In the sky, the babysitter is kind even though I'm short on cash to pay her. I pass out before I can figure out how to turn on the television.

We must become different.

Days, I watch the boats ferry from one island to the other. Nights, I watch the planes come and come and come.

The Bachelorette has teardrop earrings and the most perfect lip color known to woman.

In the city's center, people are queuing up to watch a show which the man in front of the blue wall pulled out of his hat.

What I lack in sense, I make up for in syntax.

When we were still living on the block, we developed a mice problem.
My task was to put the glue-trapped mice out of their misery with a
snow shovel.

On the avenue is a Rainbow. It's how my daughter knows to take a left.

How are we to measure time?

In intervals of space? The space between who I imagine I am and who I am; between the last time I checked my phone and the next time I'll check my phone; with teaspoons; toothpaste tubes.

If d=tr, then t must equal d divided by r, but I forget what r is.

Are you sure?

What would we do if we saw each other again?

My brother was always so good at magic. I once put on his coat and a hundred rabbits fell out of my sleeve.

The wind picks up when we stop for lobster rolls. Yi Jing asks me if life gets easier.

On the avenue, the ladies cluck at me for eating my chicken bone so clean.

It's easy to be forgotten.

It's easy to forget, especially yourself, especially in this weather.

On my last birthday, my mother sent me a card that said, "Welcome to Invisibility."

My daughters stood around me trying to stick their fingers in the cake. I asked my husband if he had ever fantasized about sleeping with a middle-aged married woman.

Oh fantasy, fantasy.

I like when he calls me wife.

My twin sister tells me that birds are so very yesteryear. Oh my faux fowl failure.

Flood.

Fled.

Flung.

Fierce.

The blue wall has been removed. Now, there's only the standing man.

I tell Yi Jing that no, it doesn't get easier. It probably gets harder, but what do I know? He leaves tomorrow for the Korean Army.

Across from me at the bar is my very prickly co-worker and his very prickly wife. They seem so tender with each other. I think I must have always been wrong about both of them.

What would it be like to do everything we're told?

S says I miss you like I miss myself. She's been painting pictures of her dead daughter.

I made a pact long ago never to call my dead son my dead son, not even in poems, especially in poems.

I call my brother whose mother is black 'my brutha from anotha mutha'. I call my brother whose mother is white but not my mother the same thing. These, I say, are my bruthas from otha muthas, then we engage in a pizza-eating contest because we all have the same father and we get our eyes and our insatiability from him.

On the avenue are sneakers and bikinis and DVDs of movies that haven't even been released. I watch a kid beat the shit out of another kid. I buy a bag of mango.

Back in the sky, my husband crawls in bed with me. He likes to leave the blinds open.

I'm always surprised when I make a good decision. It seems so unlike me. Ok, yes, seltzer. Thank you. And can I get a lime?

On weekends, we go to the country, and I try to learn the names for things: mountain laurel, Quattraporte, Sancerre.

The lady poets aren't so sure. Jane says, I need you to know that I thought you were writing in the persona of a crazy homeless person. I laugh like a crazy homeless person. Is this what you want? She asks.

Does this feel good?

What is it to have a home?

What is it to not be crazy?

Just a slice, please.

I am on the elliptical "writing poems." I send my twin sister a picture of herself in a leopard dress with a pink statue on her head. She writes back: drunk and uglee. This is how I like her.

The #diversitydude says just because you married a Korean woman don't mean you ain't a racist. I'm in the auditorium at the school. *And just because you had an Indian roommate in college don't mean you ain't a racist.*

He's all up in my face, and I'm writing on my phone. You might be a racist if:

I spray the windows with window cleaner. Helicopters fly below us. My daughters point at the streets below us. Haha! Look at our toy cars. I shit you not: I can see the Statue of Liberty from my shower.

After the applause, the man in front of the blue wall exits stage left.

In the country, I listen to the lobsters screaming when I drop them in boiling water.

Yi Jing emails asking for the A-. So very close. It was such a long winter.

We waited until spring to move downtown. On the block, mice had started gnawing through the walls. I borrowed dirty kitty litter from my pregnant friend and placed it in finger bowls in the basement. On the way to the closing my husband said, don't mention the mice. I worry that he thinks I'm a very dumb woman.

Maybe he's right. I try not to eat when hungry.

I place the bird from my lapel into an envelope and send it to my prom date in Oklahoma. I take great pleasure in knowing that it will sit unopened on his granite kitchen island.

Russell tells me I don't look old; I tell him he'll get a job soon. We eat our eggs greedily in the good sunlight.

I find the BASK card in my wallet. I imagine BASKing in Sienna in my ONE THOUSAND DOLLAR terry cloth blazer.

Just because you kissed a black boy in seventh grade don't mean you ain't a racist, but since you kissed five other boys (AND a girl) that night, it might mean you're a slut.

Dot, feather, dot.

Just because you hate the words that run through your head don't mean those words don't run through your head.

Bitch. Fat ass.

My pretty blonde daughter skims the pool. Her polka dot bikini may never fade.

Once concept becomes idea becomes thing it might as well become concept again.

On Thursday, after having watched the planes come in all night, I rise. I am all flesh. I take the elevator down to the earth. I walk west through the rubble. At the end of the avenue, I find SoulCycle (which some people say will be the END of the avenue but which I hope will be the BEGINNING of the saving of my soul). I pay $35 and choose Bike #52. For forty-five minutes, I sing and cry and sweat and pedal in darkness.

Walking home: *I'll slide right off that slick ass.*

The grandmother who is going to die soon is in the country with us. She moves in and out of stories. We don't know which ones are true, but in this one it's 3 am, and Simon has brought his horse into the truck stop.

I always thought I'd end up a waitress. I guess I still could, but I use summer as a fucking verb.

Actually, I don't, but I know people who do.

How easy it is to become complicit.

I had believed therapy would make me a better person but it only makes me more of who I am which ultimately seems like the opposite of what I was hoping to do.

The horse is standing by the deep-fryer.

Grandma says that after that Simon went out back and laid on the train tracks. She had to call a couple of men to come get him. People got drunker back then, she tells me.

The three year-old says the birds are singing the parade song. My husband says he has never seen such an unbecoming pair of shorts. Grandma points at a boat and calls it a pretty picture.

I bide my time until wine thirty.

What the seagull wants, the seagull takes.

At the beach, I try to walk off the edge of the earth. When I return, Grandma says that carloads of colored people showed up with picnic blankets. But they left. Something must have spooked them.

Boo!

I touch my husband's foot. Grandma tells us a story about a baby who died in bed then tells us we should have a son.

When things seemed to be at their worst, I got off at 42nd Street and found a meeting in a church basement in midtown. It was so depressing I decided I'd rather die in a pool of my own vomit.

2, 3, 4.

The star dogwood drops its petals while I read about my friend who talks about forgetting.

Maybe it's easier to forget in the Hamptons. Or harder. Poolside, I close my eyes and feel the slightest shift of earth.

Grandma loves the hot tub. She says, *Ok, I can die now.* We laugh.

Back at TJ's, the delphiniums dazzle.

I think I have stomach cancer but then I remember I've been popping CVS diet pills. Why not? My therapist asked. Now, I see this may have been a test. Why not for me always means: heck yeah, but maybe I'm actually supposed to consider the question.

Why not?

Why wouldn't you do this thing? What might be its consequences? What if it causes you to shit your brains out? How "important" are your "brains"?

Did you feed the fish? Brush your teeth? Change your panties? Comb your hair?

One wonders if one is trying too hard, or not hard enough.

In the sky, we are warned that if we want to make curry we should ventilate.

The man and woman who come for wine discuss what it is that makes people stink. We stare down at the world. The woman had lived in India as a graduate student so she says she's a pro.

My twin sister thought she was signing up for an affair but it was actually only one-time phone sex: this makes her feel cheap.

On the avenue is a mannequin more voluptuous than I am: this is not easy.

On the avenue, there is also a makeshift Prayer Station. I like to watch the strong bodies hold the sobbing bodies.

Come on over, honey. White people need saving too.

As an undergraduate I fell off of a turnip truck (hardy-har-har) and into Oxford, England. There, I fell for my first New York Jewish intellectual. He told me he had never met anyone from a trailer park.

Just because you've had bad sex with a New York Jewish intellectual don't make you no smarter.

When I started writing stories about my childhood, people said, But why were you being raised by a black woman?

She wasn't black, just poor.

Someone recommended I describe her skin color. Sallow, maybe? They said.

And all this time I thought white was default.

When she was raising me, I could speak in tongues.

By the time I got to Oxford, the New York Jewish intellectual translated me for the professor. What she's saying is:

I could sit by the window all day.

Mama, what are they praying for?

The richer you get the less you need God.

Did I say that?

He always seemed so embarrassed of me. Or was it ashamed?

I just don't know what to do with you, my husband says.

S is surprised that I can name the amaryllis.

My twin sister tells me that at the very moment she was contemplating a threesome, the would-be third's brother-in-law shot himself in the face in the center of the family lawn.

On the train, a heavy woman puts on drugstore mascara.

When he was a kid, my brutha from anotha mutha woke up more than once to crosses burning in his front yard.

Cue the Cackalacky blues; vomit in your mouth.

My daughters and I imagine that before shoes, people tied bark to their feet with long strips of strong grass.

In the sky, I vow to stop Instagramming sunsets.

My curated existence is so pretty. Really. I wouldn't know me if I saw me.

The blue wall may, in fact, not be blue. The man in front of it may be only an idea.

No ideas but in things.

Few things in the sky. My husband likes to keep everything minimal: three bowls: one for fruit, one for crayons, one to cry in.

Listen, I say things that aren't true.

This poem is writing itself.

The poet is walking along the avenue with the Americans. She is kneeling in the street.

She has made mistakes.

This poem is not one of those mistakes.

A white cop sits at a red table with three chairs. Yes, she can join him. No, he hasn't had to shoot anyone today. Yes, if it's this hot now, August is going to be a beast.

In the sky, my husband takes pictures of the moon as seen through the lens of his telescope. For years, he didn't read my poems.

My mother has always read my poems.

My mother has great boobs.

My mother is hilarious.

Those three lines will be her favorite lines in the book.

I love you, mom. Hi mom.

I walk the opposite way on the avenue. Everything turns green. I enter a stately building and watch a play in which a governess sits in a parlor.

Is this art?

What is art?

Is this why people are suspicious of art?

Is this why people hate art?

Do people hate art?

At least there's wine.

But I don't take any because I swore off of it this morning.

I leave five minutes early to pick the girls up from school.

Sometimes the thing that threatens to destroy us ends up saving us.

Milk, flowers. I go to the windows a thousand times a night to see the ways in which everything has changed. Night is nearly day.

On Friday, I wake up broken-hearted.

This is different from waking up hungover.

I take the broom off the hook and sweep the shards into a dustpan. I empty the shards into a brown paper bag and carry it with me on the elevator down to the avenue.

I walk along the avenue with the shards of my heart in a brown paper bag.

I walk all the way to the promenade.

I hold the bag towards the sun. I kiss it with my mouth and offer it to the sun again. I pretend the sun is Jesus. I say, not too loudly, the spirit indeed is willing but the flesh is weak. I say other things too but I say them so quietly I can't even hear them.

A cop asks me what I'm doing.

Nothing to see here, folks.

If I walk to Harlem, to Jackson Heights, to Greenpoint, to Coney Island, to that old apartment on 12th Street where I lived on imitation crabmeat and boxed Pinot Grigio, or past the city's center, all the way to the cloisters, walk and walk until my legs give out, then I might be saved.

If only from myself.

I throw the paper bag into a trash can.

I stand behind the fence at the elementary school waiting to be let in. In this scene, I am mother.

It is my best way of being. I may be a lousy wife, an impatient friend, an uneven teacher, a greedy lover, a demanding daughter, and a sloppy drunk, but I am one helluva mother.

When I was a girl, I had a seagull feather. It was my first real secret. My own mother hated how I sucked on its end so I kept it in my room and sucked it while she slept.

Or when she was away.

She was away a lot.

But when she was around she was so around.

All trains go downtown.

On the train are bodies. So many bodies. I press my arm against a stranger's.

Hi stranger. Are you reading this?

The stranger moves to the other side of the train.

At least I keep making the same mistakes. It would be disheartening to start making new ones.

My twin sister arrives before me. Her boyfriend has declared the end of his dead mother bender.

We eat kale and pork. We are middle-aged.

She asks if I ever wish I could die just for a little while.

I don't think I know what she means, I say.

But I do.

Her neighborhood feels so unlike the avenue that it makes me feel like I'm wearing a shawl. My twin sister's legs are beautiful and white, and her knee is skinned.

At Sephora, I see a short, chubby woman wearing my clothes. We wave at each other.

Bitch, fat ass.

I don't even look into SoulCycle. It's as if I'm saying: let my body and soul rot. Let me rot.

Once.

Once upon a time, a little girl was fighting a demon.

Once upon.

Once upon a time, a woman moved into the sky.

A woman turned 40, turned 41, 42, turned invisible.

Once, a woman was lost.

Once a woman was lost, it wasn't certain if she could be found.

The catch in the door made her hesitate.

Had there not been a catch in the door perhaps she never would have hesitated.

For years my mother dreamed she had killed a man and buried him in the basement. The worst part, she said, was getting caught.

The catching.

On the avenue, a man reaches for my daughter's golden hair.

A lock.

A catch.

My husband and I order Indian food. I am so grateful for this life I want to cry.

What's up? He says. You're quiet.

I imagine the trash collector, despite his rubber gloves, cutting his thumb on the shards in the brown paper bag.

I wander the sky until morning.

Oklahoma floods.

My mother drives home from her 12-hour shift at the ER.

What gets washed away?

I am an old dirt road.

Washed away, out, up.

Wish in one hand, Mama Heaton used to say.

In the other hand, you were supposed to shit.

Which gets full faster?

I dream I lose my earring, my teeth, my daughters.

I keep forgetting to watch the Bachelorette.

Apparently she doesn't find love.

But maybe she does. I'm always so bad at figuring out trailers. I always think they want me to think the opposite so they will surprise me, so I think the opposite of the opposite so I won't be surprised, but then I end up wrong.

At my deepest center, I believe TV could be my greatest salvation.

If I could just move away from the windows.

(Yes, Yi Jing, you're right: that is a fragment.)

The weekend comes, and my husband and I ferry into the city's center. We go to a beautiful place that sits on top of the water. All of the people from the gala (except for the artists) are there.

White tablecloths, white teeth.

What's it like living THERE?

Just because you live DOWNTOWN, don't mean you live DOWNTOWN.

Or, maybe I should say UP there? Waaaaaaay up there.

What's it like living?

I break bread but do not eat it. I nod. No one asks me anything so I have no secrets.

Just because you can't open your mouth don't mean your mouth don't open.

Is this a made-thing?

The water is black and pale. My hunger is palpable.

The Sancerre is supreme.

I check my phone while I pee in the fancy bathroom. PING! A text from an unknown number.

I miss you! It says.

Only women use exclamation points!

I probably miss you too, I write back, but I don't recognize your number.

Pay no attention to the drunk man behind the curtain, he writes back.

Man!?! I was wrong!!!

It is best not to engage such advances. Time might be better spent working on, say, your marriage.

But who would miss me? And exclaim it?!?

Apparently, in the last five minutes of the play which I failed to understand, everything changed. All roles were reversed. Master to servant. Poor to wealthy. The governess disappeared up a chimney.

I have no chimney.

Only a mild headache.

The clouds are high, and there are few boats in the river.

I toast waffles, pour the last of the milk, pad around in my Mrs. Callihan robe.

The petals of the delphiniums are scattered on the window sill.

Why? Asks the 3 year-old.

They're dying.

Why?

Everything dies.

What if it doesn't?

Eat your breakfast.

I wrap presents.

At the children's birthday party, the scavenger hunt ends with rainbow fans and exquisite key lime pie.

Might it all end this way?

Sunday morning on the avenue: a gentleman and me.

Our bodies gleam and are forgotten.

Nicole Callihan's poems have appeared in *PANK, Forklift, Ohio, American Poetry Review, Painted Bride Quarterly* and as a Poem-a-Day selection from the Academy of American Poets. Her books include *SuperLoop*, a collection of poems published in early 2014; *A Study in Spring*, a chapbook which she co-wrote with Zoe Ryder White and which was released in November 2015; and *The Deeply Flawed Human* which was published by Deadly Chaps Press in Summer 2016. She lives with her family in downtown Brooklyn.

Find her on the web at www.nicolecallihan.com.

CPSIA information can be obtained
at www.ICGtesting.com
Printed in the USA
BVOW08s1604060517
483183BV00001B/11/P